Book Summary:
Innovate Across Industries

"Innovate Across Industries: A Comprehensive Guide to Problem-Solving for 21st Century Success" is a visionary handbook designed to empower individuals and organizations to navigate the complex challenges of the modern world. Authored with a keen understanding of the dynamic landscapes in various industries, this book serves as a roadmap for fostering innovation that transcends sector boundaries.

Introduction:

The book opens with a compelling overview of the unique challenges that define the 21st century.

It highlights the pressing need for innovative problem-solving strategies and emphasizes the importance of embracing a cross-industry approach to achieve success in today's rapidly evolving landscape.

Chapter 1: Understanding Industry Dynamics:

Readers are guided through an insightful analysis of key industries, unraveling their intricacies and shedding light on common challenges faced across sectors. This foundational chapter sets the stage for a holistic understanding of the diverse environments in which innovation must thrive.

Chapter 2: Innovation Foundations:

Building on the industry insights, this chapter delves into the core principles of innovation. It establishes the importance of cultivating a mindset that transcends traditional industry boundaries, encouraging readers to think expansively and creatively.

Chapter 3: Case Studies in Cross-Industry Success:

Through real-world case studies, readers explore inspiring stories of organizations that have successfully embraced cross-industry innovation. These stories provide valuable lessons and practical insights, illustrating the potential for groundbreaking solutions when diverse perspectives come together.

Chapter 4: The Innovation Toolkit:

Arming readers with practical tools and techniques, this chapter equips them for creative problem-solving. From ideation to implementation, the toolkit presented here is tailored to adaptability, ensuring applicability across different industries.

Chapter 5: Collaborative Innovation:

Recognizing the power of collaboration, the book delves into strategies for building effective cross-industry partnerships. It explores the benefits of pooling collective expertise and resources, fostering an environment where innovation can thrive.

Chapter 6: Technology Integration:

In a world driven by technology, this chapter explores how to leverage technological advancements for industry-specific solutions. It addresses future-proofing strategies and provides insights into navigating the challenges presented by tech-driven industries.

Chapter 7: Overcoming Industry-Specific Challenges:

Tailoring innovation to unique industry needs, this chapter tackles sector-specific challenges. It addresses regulatory and compliance issues, offering guidance on navigating obstacles that may arise in diverse environments.

Chapter 8: Leadership in a Cross-Industry Landscape:

With a focus on leadership, this chapter guides readers in developing the skills necessary for leading diverse teams with a global perspective. It explores the qualities essential for navigating the intricacies of cross-industry landscapes.

Chapter 9: Future Trends and Emerging Industries:

Anticipating the future, the book explores emerging industries and trends. It encourages readers to prepare for unforeseen challenges, fostering a forward-thinking mindset that aligns with the ever-changing dynamics of the business world.

Conclusion:

The book concludes by recapping key takeaways and providing encouragement for continued cross-industry innovation. It emphasizes the ongoing journey of adaptation and growth, inviting readers to apply the insights gained throughout the book in their pursuit of success.

Appendices:

To further support readers, the appendices include additional resources, worksheets, and tools for practical application. These resources enhance the book's value as a comprehensive guide for those eager to innovate across industries.

"Innovate Across Industries" stands as a beacon for those seeking to thrive in the 21st century. With its blend of insightful analysis, practical tools, and inspiring stories, the book is a must-read for anyone ready to embark on a transformative journey toward innovation and success.

Introduction

Welcome to a transformative journey through "Innovate Across Industries: A Comprehensive Guide to Problem-Solving for 21st Century Success." In this chapter, we embark on a voyage into the heart of the challenges defining our dynamic era and explore the pivotal role that cross-industry innovation plays in shaping a successful future.

A. Overview of the 21st Century Challenges:

The 21st century unfolds as a landscape of unprecedented challenges and opportunities. From the rapid evolution of technology to the intricacies of global interconnectedness, individuals and organizations find themselves navigating uncharted territory.

Climate change, economic shifts, and societal transformations add layers of complexity to the fabric of our world.

In this ever-evolving environment, the need for innovative problem-solving has never been more pressing. Traditional solutions fall short in the face of dynamic challenges that transcend the boundaries of individual industries. The first section of this chapter serves as a panoramic view, offering a comprehensive overview of the multifaceted challenges that define our era.

As we delve into topics ranging from technological disruptions to socio-economic shifts, it becomes evident that a siloed approach to problem-solving is no longer sufficient. The interconnected nature of modern challenges demands a fresh perspective—one that looks beyond industry borders and embraces a holistic understanding of the complex tapestry of 21st-century issues.

B. Importance of Cross-Industry Innovation:

Enter the stage of cross-industry innovation—a paradigm that recognizes the power of collaboration and the synergy derived from diverse perspectives. The importance of this approach lies not only in its ability to address the intricacies of individual sectors but also in its capacity to spark novel solutions through the cross-pollination of ideas.

In the second part of this chapter, we unravel the significance of cross-industry innovation.

It is more than a buzzword; it is a strategic imperative for those seeking to thrive in the contemporary business landscape. By breaking down silos and fostering collaboration between traditionally distinct sectors, cross-industry innovation enables a collective response to challenges that transcend individual domains.

This book is crafted as a guide for those eager to embrace this transformative approach. Whether you're an entrepreneur, a business leader, or an aspiring innovator, the insights within these pages aim to empower you with the mindset and tools needed to navigate the complexities of the 21st century.

As we embark on this journey together, let the pages that follow be a source of inspiration and practical guidance. Through an exploration of case studies, practical tools, and collaborative strategies, we'll navigate the crossroads of challenges and innovation, equipping you to chart a course toward success in the dynamic landscape of the 21st century.

Chapter 1: Understanding Industry Dynamics

Welcome to the Heart of Innovation —a chapter dedicated to unraveling the intricacies of various industries and identifying the common challenges that bind them together. In "Understanding Industry Dynamics," we embark on a journey of exploration, analysis, and discovery to lay the foundation for effective cross-industry innovation.

A. Analysis of Key Industries:

The first section takes us deep into the diverse landscapes of key industries. From technology and healthcare to finance and manufacturing, each sector holds its unique characteristics and complexities.

Through an insightful analysis, we aim to paint a vivid picture of the challenges and opportunities that define these industries.

Technology:

In the ever-evolving world of technology, rapid advancements create both exhilarating possibilities and intricate challenges. From artificial intelligence to cybersecurity, understanding the dynamics of the tech industry is crucial for grasping the pace of innovation and disruption.

Healthcare:

The healthcare sector, with its blend of scientific advancements and human-centric challenges, presents a unique set of dynamics. Exploring topics like medical research, patient care, and healthcare infrastructure unveils the complexity inherent in this vital industry.

Finance:

Finance, the heartbeat of economic systems, operates in a landscape shaped by market fluctuations, regulatory frameworks, and technological innovations. Analyzing the financial sector sheds light on the interconnected nature of global economies.

Manufacturing:

From traditional manufacturing to the rise of smart factories, this sector is a cornerstone of industrial progress. Delving into manufacturing dynamics involves understanding supply chains, automation, and sustainability practices.

Through this analysis, we aim to cultivate a holistic understanding of the distinct challenges and opportunities within each industry. The insights gained will serve as a compass as we navigate the crossroads of cross-industry innovation.

B. Identifying Common Challenges:

While industries may seem disparate, a closer look reveals shared challenges that transcend sector boundaries. In this section, we identify and dissect these common challenges, providing a framework for approaching cross-industry problem-solving.

Innovation Resistance:

Industries, regardless of their nature, often face resistance to innovation. Whether rooted in tradition or fear of disruption, understanding and overcoming this resistance is crucial for fostering a culture of continuous improvement.

Global Interconnectedness:

The modern world operates on a global scale, and industries are increasingly interconnected. Challenges such as geopolitical shifts, supply chain disruptions, and cross-border regulations require a collaborative approach that goes beyond individual sectors.

Sustainability Imperative:

From environmental concerns to ethical business practices, sustainability is a shared challenge across industries. Navigating this imperative involves developing innovative solutions that balance economic success with social and environmental responsibility.

By identifying these common challenges, we pave the way for the chapters ahead, where we will explore strategies and tools to address them through the lens of cross-industry innovation. As we journey deeper into the book, let these insights guide you towards unlocking the potential for groundbreaking solutions that span the boundaries of individual industries.

Chapter 2: Innovation Foundations

Welcome to the bedrock of innovation—Chapter 2 unveils the foundational principles that underpin creative thinking and problem-solving. Join us in exploring the core tenets of innovation and the importance of cultivating a cross-industry mindset.

A. Principles of Innovation:

This section is a journey into the very essence of innovation, where we uncover the principles that drive transformative ideas and solutions.

Curiosity and Exploration:

Ignite the spark of innovation with an insatiable curiosity. Learn how embracing a mindset of exploration fuels the discovery of new possibilities, encouraging you to question, learn, and push the boundaries of conventional thinking.

Risk-Taking and Resilience:

Delve into the principle of calculated risk-taking. Understand how innovation often involves stepping into the unknown, and resilience becomes the key to bouncing back from setbacks, turning failures into invaluable learning experiences.

Iterative Progress:

Embrace the concept of iterative progress. Discover how innovation is often an evolving process, with each iteration bringing you closer to refined solutions. This principle emphasizes the importance of continuous improvement and adaptability.

User-Centric Focus:

Explore the significance of a user-centric approach. Learn how understanding the needs and experiences of end-users is a driving force behind successful innovation, ensuring that solutions resonate with the people they are designed to serve.

B. Establishing a Cross-Industry Mindset:

Building on the principles, this section guides you in developing a mindset that transcends the boundaries of individual industries.

Seeking Inspiration Beyond Borders:

Encourage a mindset of seeking inspiration from diverse sources. Understand how ideas from one industry can spark innovation in another, leading to the cross-pollination of concepts and the emergence of groundbreaking solutions.

Collaboration as Catalyst:

Explore the power of collaboration in cultivating a cross-industry mindset. Learn how working with individuals from different backgrounds and industries can bring fresh perspectives, fostering an environment where diverse ideas flourish.

Adaptable Thinking:

Develop the ability to think adaptably. Understand how an adaptable mindset enables you to navigate the complexities of different industries, embracing change and approaching challenges with flexibility and creativity.

Cultural Awareness and Sensitivity:

Delve into the importance of cultural awareness. Learn how understanding the cultural nuances of different industries enhances your ability to navigate diverse environments, fostering effective communication and collaboration.

As you absorb the principles of innovation and cultivate a cross-industry mindset, envision how these foundational concepts will serve as your compass in the exciting journey of cross-industry innovation. This chapter lays the groundwork for the innovative thinking that will propel you toward success in the 21st century.

Chapter 3: Case Studies in Cross-Industry Success

Welcome to a captivating exploration of triumphs and breakthroughs—Chapter 3 is a celebration of successful innovation stories that transcend industry boundaries. Join us as we examine real-world examples and distill valuable lessons learned from a spectrum of sectors, unveiling the power of cross-industry success.

A. Examining Successful Innovation Stories:

In this section, we immerse ourselves in inspiring narratives of organizations that have harnessed the potential of cross-industry innovation to achieve remarkable success.

Healthcare Meets Technology:

Explore how the collaboration between healthcare and technology gave rise to groundbreaking solutions. From wearable health devices to telemedicine platforms, witness the transformative impact of merging medical expertise with cutting-edge technological advancements.

Finance and Sustainable Practices:

Delve into case studies where the finance industry embraced sustainability. From green investments to ethical banking practices, discover how financial institutions have integrated environmental responsibility into their core strategies, demonstrating the positive outcomes of cross-industry collaboration.

Manufacturing and Design Thinking:

Uncover how the marriage of manufacturing and design thinking has revolutionized product development. From user-centered design in the automotive industry to incorporating sustainability principles in manufacturing processes, witness how innovation flourishes at the intersection of diverse disciplines.

These stories serve as beacons of inspiration, illustrating the potential for groundbreaking solutions when industries collaborate and share insights. Each success story is a testament to the transformative power of cross-industry innovation.

B. Lessons Learned from Varied Sectors:

As we navigate these case studies, it's essential to distill the lessons learned—universal principles that can be applied across a multitude of sectors.

Lesson 1: Embrace Diversity of Thought:

Discover how embracing diverse perspectives fuels innovation. Organizations that actively seek input from different industries and backgrounds cultivate a rich pool of ideas, driving creative problem-solving.

Lesson 2: Foster Collaborative Culture:

Explore how successful cross-industry innovators foster a collaborative culture. By breaking down silos and promoting open communication, they create environments where diverse teams can thrive and bring their unique strengths to the table.

Lesson 3: Stay Agile and Adaptable:

Witness the importance of agility in the face of change. Industries that remain flexible and adaptable can more effectively navigate the evolving landscape, responding to challenges with resilience and innovation.

As we conclude this chapter, let these case studies and lessons learned be a source of inspiration and guidance. The journey ahead will build upon these foundations, equipping you with the insights and tools needed to foster your own cross-industry success stories.

Chapter 4: The Innovation Toolkit

Welcome to a workshop of creativity and adaptability—Chapter 4 is your guide to the essential elements of innovation. Let's delve into "The Innovation Toolkit," where we explore a variety of tools and techniques for creative problem-solving, along with strategies to adapt these approaches to the unique demands of different industries.

A. Tools and Techniques for Creative Problem-Solving:

This section opens the door to a treasure trove of tools designed to spark innovation and tackle challenges from fresh perspectives.

Design Thinking:

Embark on the journey of design thinking—an empathetic, user-centric approach to problem-solving. Learn how empathy maps, brainstorming sessions, and prototyping can be harnessed to uncover novel solutions, fostering innovation across industries.

Mind Mapping:

Unlock the power of visual thinking with mind mapping. Discover how this technique helps organize thoughts, identify connections, and stimulate creativity, providing a versatile tool applicable to a range of challenges in diverse sectors.

SWOT Analysis:

Navigate strategic decision-making with the classic SWOT analysis. Understand how strengths, weaknesses, opportunities, and threats can be systematically evaluated to inform business strategies and drive innovation in various industries.

Divergent and Convergent Thinking:

Explore the dynamic interplay between divergent and convergent thinking. Learn how to generate a multitude of ideas (divergent) and then refine them into practical solutions (convergent), fostering a balanced approach to problem-solving.

As you immerse yourself in these tools, envision how they can be tailored to your unique challenges, sparking creativity and innovation within your specific industry.

B. Adaptability Strategies for Different Industries:

Building on the tools introduced, this section explores adaptability strategies to ensure that your innovation toolkit remains effective across diverse industries.

Customization for Healthcare:

Understand how to customize your approach for the healthcare sector. Adapt tools like design thinking to address patient-centric challenges, ensuring that innovations align with the unique demands and ethical considerations of the healthcare industry.

Agility in Technology:

Explore strategies for maintaining agility in the ever-evolving landscape of technology. Learn how to integrate rapid prototyping and iterative development cycles, enabling technology-driven industries to stay ahead in the innovation game.

Sustainability Integration:

Discover how to infuse sustainability into your innovation toolkit. Adapt tools like SWOT analysis to assess the environmental impact of strategies, ensuring that sustainability remains a core consideration across various industries.

These adaptability strategies serve as a bridge, connecting the general principles of creative problem-solving with the specific needs of different industries. As we conclude this chapter, envision how these tools and adaptability strategies can empower you to navigate the complex terrain of cross-industry innovation, bringing your ideas to life in dynamic and transformative ways.

Chapter 5: Collaborative Innovation

Step into the realm of synergy and collective genius—Chapter 5 is an exploration of collaborative innovation, where we dive into the intricacies of building cross-industry partnerships and leveraging the collective expertise of diverse teams.

A. Building Cross-Industry Partnerships:

This section is a guide on how to foster collaboration between industries, unlocking the potential for shared insights and mutual growth.

Identifying Strategic Alliances:

Learn the art of identifying strategic partners from different industries. Understand how aligning with organizations that complement your strengths and bring unique perspectives can amplify your innovation efforts, creating a synergy that goes beyond individual capabilities.

Cultivating Open Communication:

Explore the importance of open communication in cross-industry partnerships. Discover how transparent and collaborative communication fosters an environment where ideas can flow freely, breaking down silos and creating a foundation for fruitful collaboration.

Building Multidisciplinary Teams:

Explore the benefits of assembling multidisciplinary teams. Learn how diverse skill sets and perspectives contribute to a richer pool of ideas, fostering innovation that draws from the collective expertise of individuals with varied backgrounds.

Cross-Training and Skill Exchange:

Delve into the practice of cross-training and skill exchange. Understand how exposing team members to different industries and skill sets enhances their adaptability and creativity, breaking down barriers between disciplines and encouraging a holistic approach to problem-solving.

Creating a Culture of Inclusivity:

Uncover the importance of creating a culture of inclusivity within collaborative teams. Learn how embracing diversity and promoting an inclusive environment fosters a sense of belonging, empowering team members to share their unique expertise and perspectives without reservation.

As we navigate this chapter, envision how the principles of collaborative innovation can become a driving force within your endeavors. By building cross-industry partnerships and leveraging collective expertise, you embark on a journey where the sum is truly greater than its parts. The collaborative spirit laid out in this chapter is a beacon guiding you toward innovative solutions that transcend industry boundaries.

Chapter 6: Technology Integration

Welcome to the nexus of innovation and technology—Chapter 6 is your guide to seamlessly integrate technological advancements into industry solutions. Join us as we explore the art of harnessing technology for transformative purposes and discover future-proofing strategies for industries navigating the ever-evolving tech landscape.

A. Harnessing Technology for Industry Solutions:

In this section, we immerse ourselves in the dynamic world of technology, uncovering ways to leverage its power for industry-specific solutions.

Data-Driven Decision Making:

Explore the realm of data-driven decision-making. Learn how industries can harness the vast amounts of data at their disposal to gain insights, optimize processes, and make informed decisions that drive innovation and efficiency.

Automation and Efficiency:

Delve into the integration of automation to enhance efficiency. From manufacturing processes to customer service, understand how embracing automation can streamline operations, reduce costs, and pave the way for more innovative practices.

Emerging Technologies:

Embark on a journey through emerging technologies. From artificial intelligence to blockchain and the Internet of Things, discover how these transformative technologies have the potential to reshape industries, creating new possibilities and driving unprecedented innovation.

B. Future-Proofing Strategies for Tech-Driven Industries:

This section is a strategic exploration of future-proofing techniques, ensuring that tech-driven industries stay ahead of the curve.

Continuous Learning and Adaptation:

Understand the importance of continuous learning and adaptation in tech-driven industries. Explore strategies for staying updated on technological advancements, fostering a culture of innovation that embraces change rather than resists it.

Sustainability in Tech:

Delve into the integration of sustainability principles within technology-driven sectors. Learn how industries can balance the rapid pace of technological innovation with ethical considerations and environmental responsibility, ensuring a sustainable and responsible approach to growth.

Agile Development and Scalability:

Explore the concepts of agile development and scalability. Understand how adopting agile methodologies allows tech-driven industries to respond swiftly to changes, while scalability ensures that innovative solutions can be adapted and expanded as needed.

As we conclude this chapter, envision the transformative potential that technology holds for your industry. By harnessing its power and adopting future-proofing strategies, you position yourself on the cutting edge of innovation. The intersection of technology and industry solutions is a landscape of limitless possibilities, waiting to be explored and harnessed for the benefit of your organization and the broader world.

Chapter 7: Overcoming Industry-Specific Challenges

Welcome to the heart of targeted innovation—Chapter 7 is your guide to navigating the unique challenges that each industry presents. Join us as we explore the art of tailoring innovation for specific sectors and address the intricate landscape of regulatory and compliance issues.

A. Tailoring Innovation for Unique Sectors:

In this section, we embark on a journey of understanding the intricacies of various industries and tailoring innovative solutions to meet their specific needs.

Healthcare and Personalized Solutions:

Delve into the healthcare sector, where the emphasis on personalized care drives innovation. Explore how technologies like genomics and telemedicine cater to individual health needs, fostering a patient-centric approach to healthcare solutions.

Finance and Fintech Revolution:

Uncover the challenges in the finance sector and the ongoing fintech revolution. Explore how innovations such as blockchain, robo-advisors, and digital currencies are reshaping financial landscapes, offering solutions that balance security, accessibility, and efficiency.

Manufacturing and Sustainable Practices:

Explore the challenges faced by the manufacturing industry and the integration of sustainable practices. Learn how innovative solutions, such as circular economy models and eco-friendly production processes, address environmental concerns while enhancing efficiency.

B. Addressing Regulatory and Compliance Issues:

This section is a strategic exploration of addressing the complex terrain of regulatory and compliance issues that industries must navigate.

Navigating Healthcare Regulations:

Understand the intricacies of healthcare regulations and compliance. Explore how innovation can be tailored to adhere to strict regulatory standards, ensuring that advancements in healthcare are ethically sound and meet the highest standards of safety and efficacy.

Financial Compliance in Fintech:

Delve into the world of financial compliance, particularly within the dynamic fintech space. Learn how technologies like RegTech are revolutionizing compliance processes, ensuring that financial innovations align with regulatory frameworks and industry standards.

Manufacturing Standards and Eco-Friendly Practices:

Explore how the manufacturing sector addresses regulatory standards and compliance with environmental practices. Discover how innovative solutions help industries meet stringent regulations, fostering a balance between economic viability and responsible environmental stewardship.

As we conclude this chapter, envision how tailoring innovation to industry-specific challenges and addressing regulatory issues can pave the way for transformative solutions. By understanding the unique needs and constraints of different sectors, you position yourself to overcome challenges and drive meaningful change. The journey ahead involves navigating the delicate balance between innovation and compliance, ensuring that your solutions are not only groundbreaking but also ethically and legally sound.

Chapter 8: Leadership in a Cross-Industry Landscape

Welcome to the helm of innovation—Chapter 8 is a guide to effective leadership in a cross-industry landscape. Join us as we explore the art of developing leaders with a global perspective and strategies for leading diverse teams toward success.

A. Developing Leaders with a Global Perspective:

In this section, we delve into the principles and practices necessary to nurture leaders with a global perspective, equipped to navigate the complexities of a cross-industry landscape.

Embracing Cultural Intelligence:

Explore the concept of cultural intelligence (CQ) and its role in developing leaders with a global mindset. Learn how embracing diverse cultural perspectives enhances leadership effectiveness, fostering a global understanding that transcends geographical and industry boundaries.

Continuous Learning and Adaptation:

Understand the importance of continuous learning and adaptation for leaders in a cross-industry context. Explore strategies for staying informed about global trends, technological advancements, and industry shifts, ensuring leaders remain agile and proactive in their decision-making.

Encouraging Collaborative Leadership:

Delve into the practice of collaborative leadership. Learn how fostering a culture of collaboration and shared leadership empowers individuals from different industries to contribute their unique strengths, driving innovation and success on a global scale.

B. Strategies for Leading Diverse Teams:

This section is a strategic exploration of leading diverse teams, emphasizing the skills and approaches necessary to harness the full potential of cross-functional collaboration.

Inclusive Leadership Practices:

Explore the principles of inclusive leadership. Learn how creating an inclusive environment fosters a sense of belonging, encourages diverse perspectives, and unleashes the full creative potential of teams representing various industries and backgrounds.

Effective Communication Across Borders:

Understand the nuances of effective communication in a cross-industry context. Explore strategies for overcoming language barriers, time zone differences, and cultural variations, ensuring that communication remains clear, inclusive, and conducive to collaboration.

Adaptable Leadership Style:

Delve into the importance of an adaptable leadership style. Learn how leaders can tailor their approach to different individuals and situations, recognizing the unique dynamics of diverse teams and industries to foster a collaborative and harmonious work environment.

As we conclude this chapter, envision the transformative impact that effective leadership can have on cross-industry innovation. By developing leaders with a global perspective and implementing strategies for leading diverse teams, you pave the way for a dynamic and inclusive organizational culture that thrives on the richness of diversity and the power of collaboration.

The journey ahead involves not only navigating the complexities of industries but also inspiring and guiding diverse teams toward shared success.

Chapter 9: Future Trends and Emerging Industries

Welcome to the horizon of possibilities—Chapter 9 is your guide to anticipating future trends and navigating the uncharted territories of emerging industries. Join us as we explore the art of foreseeing the next wave of industries and preparing for unforeseen challenges on the horizon.

A. Anticipating the Next Wave of Industries:

In this section, we embark on a journey of foresight, exploring strategies to identify and anticipate the industries that will shape the future.

Trend Analysis and Market Research:

Delve into the world of trend analysis and market research. Understand how staying informed about technological advancements, societal shifts, and economic developments can provide insights into the industries poised for growth, helping you position your organization at the forefront of innovation.

Networking and Industry Insights
:
Explore the power of networking and industry insights. Learn how building connections with thought leaders, participating in conferences, and engaging in cross-industry collaborations can offer a firsthand understanding of emerging trends, enabling you to adapt proactively to the evolving business landscape.

Scenario Planning for Future Industries:

Understand the value of scenario planning. Explore how creating potential future scenarios and evaluating their impact on industries can assist in developing strategies that are flexible and resilient, ensuring your organization is prepared for various possible outcomes.

B. Preparing for Unforeseen Challenges:

This section is a strategic exploration of preparing for challenges that may emerge unexpectedly, ensuring resilience and adaptability in the face of uncertainty.

Risk Management Strategies:

Delve into risk management strategies. Learn how anticipating potential challenges, assessing their impact, and developing mitigation plans can enhance your organization's ability to navigate unforeseen obstacles, fostering a culture of resilience and preparedness.

Agile Organizational Structures:

Explore the concept of agile organizational structures. Understand how fostering flexibility and adaptability within your organization allows for swift responses to unforeseen challenges, promoting innovation and ensuring that your teams can pivot effectively when faced with unexpected disruptions.

Crisis Communication and Leadership:

Delve into the art of crisis communication and leadership. Learn how transparent and effective communication, coupled with strong leadership, can guide your organization through unforeseen challenges, maintaining trust and morale within your teams.

As we conclude this chapter, envision the future landscape of industries and the dynamic challenges that may lie ahead. By anticipating trends and preparing for the unforeseen, you position yourself to not only navigate change but to embrace it as an opportunity for growth and innovation.

The journey ahead involves not only staying ahead of emerging trends but also fostering a resilient and adaptable organizational culture that can thrive amidst uncertainty.

Conclusion: Navigating the Crossroads of Innovation

As we conclude our journey through "Innovate Across Industries: A Comprehensive Guide to Problem-Solving for 21st Century Success," it's time to reflect on the insights gained and look ahead with a sense of anticipation for the transformative possibilities that lie on the horizon.

A. Recap of Key Takeaways:

In this comprehensive guide, we've explored the multifaceted landscape of cross-industry innovation, uncovering principles and strategies to thrive in the dynamic 21st century. Let's recap some key takeaways:

Understanding Industry Dynamics: We delved into the intricacies of various industries, identifying common challenges and laying the foundation for cross-industry problem-solving.

Innovation Foundations: Cultivating a mindset rooted in curiosity, risk-taking, and user-centric focus forms the bedrock of successful innovation.

Collaborative Innovation: Building cross-industry partnerships and leveraging collective expertise emerged as powerful tools for driving innovation.

Technology Integration: Harnessing technology and adopting future-proofing strategies position industries at the forefront of innovation.

Overcoming Industry-Specific Challenges: Tailoring solutions to unique sectors and navigating regulatory issues are essential for successful cross-industry endeavors.

Leadership in a Cross-Industry Landscape: Developing leaders with a global perspective and leading diverse teams foster an environment conducive to innovation.

Future Trends and Emerging Industries: Anticipating the next wave of industries and preparing for unforeseen challenges are crucial for staying ahead in the ever-evolving business landscape.

B. Encouragement for Continued Cross-Industry Innovation:

As we conclude this guide, let the journey we've undertaken be a source of inspiration and motivation. Cross-industry innovation is not just a strategy; it's a mindset—an approach that recognizes the interconnectedness of our world and the boundless potential that arises when diverse perspectives converge.

Cross-industry innovation is an ongoing process, and the challenges of tomorrow will require the adaptability and creativity that this guide has instilled. Encourage your teams to embrace change, to seek inspiration beyond familiar borders, and to build partnerships that transcend industry lines.

Remember, innovation is not a destination but a continuous journey. The future holds unknown opportunities and challenges, and your ability to navigate them will be shaped by the principles and strategies we've explored together.

In the spirit of continuous improvement and collaboration, let this guide be a companion in your quest for innovation. May your endeavors be marked by creativity, resilience, and a steadfast commitment to making a positive impact across industries.

Here's to a future filled with groundbreaking solutions, transformative collaborations, and the ongoing pursuit of excellence in the ever-evolving landscape of the 21st century.

Remember, innovation is not a destination but a continuous journey. The future holds unknown opportunities and challenges, and your ability to navigate them will be shaped by the principles and strategies we've explored together.

In the spirit of continuous improvement and collaboration, let this guide be a companion in your quest for innovation. May your endeavors be marked by creativity, resilience, and a steadfast commitment to making a positive impact across industries.

Here's to a future filled with groundbreaking solutions, transformative collaborations, and the ongoing pursuit of excellence in the ever-evolving landscape of the 21st century.

Appendices: Resources and Practical Tools

Welcome to the appendices—an invaluable section providing additional resources and practical tools to enhance your journey in cross-industry innovation. Here, you'll find a wealth of information to deepen your understanding and facilitate the practical application of the concepts explored in this guide.

A. Additional Resources:

Recommended Reading List: Explore a curated list of books, articles, and research papers that delve deeper into the realms of innovation, leadership, and cross-industry collaboration. These resources are handpicked to complement and extend your knowledge beyond the scope of this guide.

Online Learning Platforms: Access links to reputable online learning platforms offering courses on innovation, design thinking, and industry-specific trends. These platforms provide an interactive learning experience, allowing you to further hone your skills at your own pace.

Industry Reports and Insights: Stay informed about the latest trends and challenges in specific industries through industry reports and insights. Access reputable sources that provide in-depth analyses and forecasts, keeping you ahead of the curve in cross-industry innovation.

B. Worksheets and Tools for Practical Application:

Design Thinking Templates:
Download templates for design thinking processes, including empathy maps, journey maps, and ideation canvases. These tools facilitate a structured approach to creative problem-solving, aiding you in generating innovative solutions.

SWOT Analysis Worksheets:
Utilize customizable SWOT analysis worksheets for different industries. These tools guide you through the process of identifying strengths, weaknesses, opportunities, and threats, providing a strategic framework for cross-industry innovation.

Scenario Planning Guides:

Explore guides and templates for scenario planning, allowing you to envision potential future scenarios and prepare your organization for various outcomes. These resources enhance your strategic preparedness in the face of uncertainty.

Leadership Development Plans: Develop personalized leadership development plans using templates that outline goals, strategies, and actionable steps. These tools support the cultivation of leaders with a global perspective and the ability to lead diverse teams effectively.

As you explore these appendices, consider them as companions on your journey toward cross-industry innovation. The resources and tools provided are meant to empower you, offering practical guidance and a tangible framework for applying the principles discussed in this guide. May these appendices serve as valuable assets in your ongoing pursuit of innovation and success in the 21st century.

www.ingramcontent.com/pod-product-compliance
Lightning Source LLC
Chambersburg PA
CBHW052039280526
45791CB00010B/3010